Lee Sanders Pratt, Newton Bateman, Clark E. Carr

Galesburg Sketches - Specimen Bits

a few of Galesburg's contributions to contemporary literature

Lee Sanders Pratt, Newton Bateman, Clark E. Carr

Galesburg Sketches - Specimen Bits
a few of Galesburg's contributions to contemporary literature

ISBN/EAN: 9783337090388

Printed in Europe, USA, Canada, Australia, Japan

Cover: Foto ©Andreas Hilbeck / pixelio.de

More available books at **www.hansebooks.com**

Galesburg Sketches

SPECIMEN BITS

✢ A few of Galesburg's Contributions to Contemporary Literature Here first Embodied and Put forth as a Partial Expression of the Literary Talent of the College City ✢ ✢ ✢ ✢ ✢ ✢ ✢

GALESBURG ILLINOIS
MDCCCXCVII

Knox Edition

I would adopt as my message to the dear students of Knox, the impressive words of Paul, in his message to the Philippians: "Whatsoever things are true, whatsoever things are honest, whatsoever things are just, whatsoever things are pure, whatsoever things are lovely, whatsoever things are of good report, think on these things."

Newton Bateman.

Copyright, 1897,
By LEE SANDERS PRATT

Editor: LEE SANDERS PRATT

> "Call him, if you please, a bookmaker, not an author."—*Voltaire.*

Contributors:

> "Why did I write? What sin to me unknown
> Dipt me in ink, my parents' or my own?"
> —*Pope.*

Publishers: THE WAGONER-MEHLER CO.

> "Though an angel should write,
> Still 'tis devils must print."
> —*Tom Moore.*

Distributor: THE CAREY BOOK STORE

> "A merchant of great traffic through the world."
> —*Shakespeare.*

Buyers:

> "I would earnestly advise them, FOR THEIR GOOD, to order this book to be punctually served up."—*Addison.*

INTRODUCTION

*"O wad some Power the giftie gie us
To see oursel's as ithers see us."*

THIS VOLUME is the answer to that prayer. In glad surprise has our sight been greeted, from time to time, with familiar home-names in periodicals coming to us from distant cities, subscribing a poem in graceful guise, a classic tale, a song or lettered page of surpassing beauty. But what profit that a melodious chord be struck here and there to vibrate for a moment on the sated ear of indifference and then, unsustained, to die into silence,—cui bono? Why not, rather, unite these scattered strains into a symphony that should delight the ear and touch the heart of those who know and love the singers?

Herein lies the raison d'etre of the little book to which this page is the simple introduction. It is an attempt to gather and set forth in one collation a portion of the rich literary fruitage of our fair city,—incomplete, to be sure, but perhaps in sufficient abundance to cheer our authors with the heartening thought that here exists a true fellowship of letters, a literary coterie of no mean order. And may our little band "take heart of grace" from this look into one another's faces, this grasp of congenial hands. So shall it be that, favorably as the city is already known for the excellence of its work in current literature, the publication of these "Specimen Bits" will mark a new epoch in our literary history.

If we can, then, recognize in this garnered sheaf something of the beauty and merit which others have often observed in our single flowers of thought, when they grew and blossomed apart, the "giftie" will not have been bestowed in vain.

Excerpts from Various Lectures by Dr. Bateman Referring to Knox College and its Students

✛ The three following pages are dedicated to Knox College, with the hope and prayer that these words of Dr. Bateman, that beautiful and gentle spirit whose life was an inspiration and a benediction, may incite his "dear boys and girls" to higher and nobler living and to more earnest devotion to the College that he loved. ✛

Closing Page of a Lecture entitled "Knox College"

Delivered in chapel, "Sept. 7, 1893"

Give to this noble school your loving confidence—she is worthy of it. Give her your active influence she needs it. Speak, write, work for her; rally around her; do what you can for her. For thus you, her literary children, can do more for her speedy enlargement than all other forces combined.

From a Lecture entitled "Suggestions to Students"

Given in chapel, "Sept. 6, 1888"

This is a *Christian* College in the broad, catholic, blessed and precious sense of the word. We joyfully recognize and earnestly seek to honor and enthrone here the God of Heaven and His Son, Jesus Christ, and the sublime precepts and principles of the Christian religion.

IN SPEAKING OF THE MORNING CHAPEL SERVICES:

We come here to meet our Father in Heaven, the Maker of all things, and Him who is the Way and the Truth and the Life. We come as worshippers, and for the time being this is none other than the house of God. But I would that when we come hither, to seek our Heavenly Father's blessing for the day, we might all feel a certain softening and subduing influence stealing over us, a certain presence belonging to the place, stilling the tumult of our thoughts and bringing to our hearts that sweet receptive hush, in which the voice of conscience, which is none other than the voice of God in the soul, may be heard. God will surely bless—does always bless—every such willing and waiting heart. No student can spend the few allotted moments of this service in such a frame of mind, without feeling the hallowed touch of an unseen but gracious hand upon the chords of his heart, without hearing the soft, sweet call of heavenly voices bidding him live a truer, manlier, nobler, holier life, without being uplifted, calmed and strengthened. And he will go to his recitations and studies clearer in mental vision, stronger in worthy purposes, and braver and happier in heart.

It is "lovely and of good report," always and in all things to be mindful of the feelings and of the comfort and convenience of others with whom we are associated,—that is, to do to them as we would that they should do to us in like circumstances. Taking, then, along with us the Golden Rule that He has given us, let us see how like an angel monitor it will follow us everywhere, through and about this building and these grounds, leaving peace and order and sunshine in its path.

THE CLOSING WORDS OF THE LECTURE:

And so, all day and every day, if we will only *think*, we shall be sure to do those "things which are lovely and of good report,"—becoming more courteous, more refined, nobler types of what the amenities of culture can do; more thoughtful, more mindful of others, worthier representatives of this Christian college.

From a Lecture
" Advice to Students "

Given in chapel, " Sept. 4, 1890 "

Begin right, and keep right, and hold on and hold out, to the end. Do not relax your grasp, do not grow careless, do not think it a little matter to slur over a lesson, to cut a recitation, to shirk a college duty, now and then. It is not a little matter,—it is the beginning of a habit which, if not checked, will steadily and rapidly increase.

The brightest, gladdest, happiest persons I know are the college boys and girls who are conscious of trying to do their whole duty.

From a Lecture entitled
"The True Strength of Colleges"

Given "Thursday, Nov. 6, 1884"

Christ and culture, religion and learning, nature and revelation, the works and word of God, these are the legends inscribed on these walls, the principles that hold sway in the beliefs and teachings of this School. Sound learning and a pure faith, the life that now is, and also that which is to come, the temporal and the eternal, the seen and the unseen,— these are some of the watchwords of Knox College, some of the pairs of fundamental truths which here have glad and hearty recognition.

From Two
California Lectures

SPEAKING OF THE FAREWELL SCENE AT THE GALESBURG
DEPOT WHEN HE WAS SETTING OUT ON HIS
JOURNEY TO CALIFORNIA:

And there, too, were some of the class of '78, my own boys, God bless them. Did ever teacher have such boys and girls as I have had and still have, in Knox College, anyway? They are just a solid comfort.

SPEAKING OF THE REV. DR. WARREN, OF SAN MATEO,
A GRADUATE OF KNOX COLLEGE, OF
THE CLASS OF '47:

He was full of interest in and inquiries about his Alma Mater, and upon my telling him how well we were getting along and what a glorious company of lads and lassies we had here, he proposed that his daughter should play and we all sing that glorious battle-hymn of ours,

"Here's to Good Old Knox."

The young lady stepped to the piano, and we sang till the San Mateo hills fairly rang again; and with that song, identified with an institution whose welfare is my daily and nightly thought, for a benediction, we exchanged good nights.

TABLE OF CONTENTS:

		Pages.
ENTREE - - - -		10
TRIBUTE TO THE FLAG		
HOW I GOT THE OUTSIDE SEAT	*Newton Bateman* -	11-18
VERSES		
IN HISTORIC DALECARLIA -	*Hjalmar Sundquist* -	19-21
A VISION OF SANTA CLAUS -	*Philip G. Wright* -	22-23
A LULLABY - -	*Marie Zetterberg* -	24-25
THE PLAINT OF THE LEAVES -	*John Huston Finley* -	26
THE SCARF OF THE DEMOISELLE	*Mary C. Hurd* -	27-30
"PITTYPAT AND TIPPYTOE" -	*Clara Gordon Coulson*	31-35
THE BROWNIES ON OUR STREET	*Elizabeth Clark* -	36-37
LITTLE THINGS - -	*Julia Fletcher Carney*	38
LINCOLN AT GETTYSBURG -	*Clark E. Carr* -	39-40
AN EVERGREEN - -	*Helena Crumett-Lee* -	41-45
THE PASSING OF CADMUS -	*Earnest Elmo Calkins*	46-48
THE FIR TREE - -	*Alice B. Cushing* -	49-51
THE METEOR - -	*Frank Hinckley Sisson*	52
A REVERIE BY THE HEATHER	*Janet Greig* -	53-54
TO THE DAISY - -	*Marie Zetterberg* -	55
AN IMMORTELLE -	*Annie Bateman Ewart*	56-57
THE HOME COMING OF THORSTEIN ERICSSON		
- -	*Wm. E. Simonds* -	58-67
LITTLE FOOTSTEPS -	*Lee S. Pratt* -	68
THE SUN'S WOOING -	*Wm. F. Bentley* -	69-71
GALESBURG'S MILTONS -	- -	72
NOTES - - -	-	73-76

Tribute to the Flag.

The true American patriot is ever a worshipper. The Starry Symbol of his country's Sovereignty is to him radiant with a diviner glory than that which meets his mortal vision. It epitomizes the splendid results of dreary ages of experiments & failures in human government. As he gazes upon its starry folds, undulating responsive to the whispering winds of the upper air, it sometimes seems to his rapt spirit to recede, further & further into the soft blue skies, till the heavens open, and angel hands plant it upon the battlements of Paradise.

Wherever that Ensign floats, on the land or on the sea, it is to him the very Shekinah of his political love & faith, luminous with the presence of that God who conducted his fathers across the sea, & through the perils of the wilderness & the fires of the Revolution, to the Pisgah heights of civil & religious liberty. Its stars seem real — its lines of white symbol the family of his heroic Sires — those of red, their patriot blood shed in defense of the right. To defend that flag is to him something more than a duty — it is a joy, a coveted privilege, akin to that which nerves the arm & directs the blow in defence of home & wife & child. To insult it is worse than infamy — to make war upon it, more than treason.

Dr. Bateman.

HOW I GOT THE OUTSIDE SEAT

A MEMORABLE episode of my stay on the Pacific coast was a visit to Pescadero, some seventy-five miles from San Francisco. The route is by the cars of the Southern Pacific to San Mateo, thence by stage to Pescadero, about thirty-five miles away.

Having received timely notice of the desirableness of securing an *outside* seat, and of the rush there would be for that coveted advantage upon the arrival of the train at San Mateo, I was ready for action. As the train was being "slowed up" to the station, I was on the lowest step of the platform, satchel in hand, ready for a spring. The moment we reached the first end of the platform I leaped ashore and made for the stages, which were in plain sight on the hill some two hundred yards away. Now, two hundred yards was precisely the length of the course on which I had made my best and most famous time in my racing days when in college; and as my eye measured the distance and took in the situation—as the value of the prize of victory, (an outside seat for a six hours' ride over one of the finest mountain roads in California), came into the field of mental vision—as I thought of the laurels I had won, time and again, over that two-hundred-yard stadium in Illinois College, (for, incredible as it may seem to you long-metre gentlemen that a man of such Zacchean altitude should achieve renown as a runner, I do assure you that I wore that champion-belt for nearly two years over one hundred and sixty competitors)– as Vergil's account of the last magnificent spurt made by old Entellus in his boxing bout with the boasting Dares, came to my mind, (and here you see one of the many incidental benefits of classical study)—as I thought of "Good old Knox," and that for the time being her honor and prestige were in my especial keeping, and that they must and should be sustained—and as I thought of the keen delight it would be to tell the story, if peradventure I should succeed—as these thoughts and memories, and other thronging visions and fancies flashed through my brain in a millionth part of the time it has taken to write them, I resolved to *reach those stages in advance of all other persons*, of whatsoever race, age, color, sex, or previous condition. And the way this chronicler, (for, alas, there is no other historian to record the deed and send it to posterity and glory)— the way this chronicler did pick up and put down his feet for the next two or three minutes would have filled even you winged young Mercuries, (please notice another classical reference); would have filled even you swift-footed Hectors, (again, as I live; you must excuse me, there is such a fascination about Homer and Vergil—they are such an unwasting source of telling metaphors and matchless tropes and similes); would have filled even you, (there now, I have cut loose from Greece and Rome at last)—would have filled *even you*, familiar as you are with feats of prowess and daring, with astonishment, perchance with envy.

The slight advantage I had secured by being ready to jump ashore the moment the train came alongside the platform, was improved to the utmost. Looking over my shoulder, I saw my competitors in the race, seven men and three women, sweeping after me and converging towards the common goal—the stages. It became evident, in a moment, that my most dangerous rivals were two men and a woman, who were pressing me hard. The woman was a very Anne of Geierstein for fleetness and endurance; she ran like a deer, while her laughter rang out in the most mocking and contagious manner—though I must confess that I had other uses for all *my* breath just then. A moment more and she had left the two men behind and was actually gaining on the Galesburg athlete! Must he, then, be beaten at last, and by a woman? Perish the thought! But what was to be done? She was already so near that the very color of her ribbons and eyes was plainly discernible, and, alas, she was gaining fast. But one recourse was left me; I hated to resort to it, but hated more to be beaten, for by this time the others had given up the contest and the air was filled with shouts from the crowds on the platform and about the stages as they witnessed the race. So when within about fifty feet of the stages I threw away my valise, made a last desperate spurt, and got in ahead and secured the coveted outside seats. You should have heard that unconscionable damsel's shout of derisive laughter when that valise had to go! The whole thing was an unexpected and rare bit of fun, hugely enjoyed both by participants and spectators, one of the latter of whom was heard to remark that he "never saw a man of *eighty* run like that before."

  I was on my way to visit a college classmate living in Pescadero, whom I had not seen for many years. His daughter had joined me in San Francisco and was going home for a brief vacation. She knew of my purpose to secure, at all reasonable hazards, outside seats for us both, and had witnessed the race as she came slowly on. In a few moments she arrived at the stages, bringing that forlorn looking valise, and radiant with delight at the brilliant triumph of her father's old college chum.

I had been but just in time. The two seats I had secured were the only outside ones left in the two mountain stages. To admit a third with us would require a *little crowding*, but when I saw the wistful face of the brave little woman who came so near to spoiling this story, as she was about entering one of the coaches there to be imprisoned for six hours, I held a brief consultation with my protege, and we unanimously decided to invite the lady to share our seat on the hurricane deck of the stage. She accepted, with thanks. In genuine western style, we severally introduced ourselves, and a most agreeable and entertaining travelling companion she proved to be.

NEWTON BATEMAN.

LIFE THOUGHTS FROM DR. BATEMAN.

FOR "THE QUIET HOUR":

"The more complete our isolation, the more profound should be our listening,—assured that the divine lips are ever close to our ears with a message. This is just the way the great and good have ascended the heights of a faith on which the peace of God abides forever."

FOR CRISES IN LIFE:

"See to it that as you come to the great moral dividing ridges of life, the solemn moments of choice, you turn your faces toward the sunrise, not toward the sunset."

Verses Penned at Pebble Beach, California

Oh sobbing sea—oh moaning sea!
What bitter anguish grieveth thee?
Why goes the sound of wailing waves
Resounding through thy hollow caves?
Why dost thou rise in threatening wrath,
When angry tempests cross thy path—
Aiming thy helpless wrath so high,
Against the armies of the sky?

I, too, in wistful yearning wail,
Because my hopes and longings fail—
Because my cherished plans are lost,
With all the labor they had cost.
And, when the adverse storms arise,
I vent my wrath against the skies,
And waste my strength in bitterness
That does not make my burden less.

Oh smiling sea—oh tender sea!
What wondrous beauty covers thee!
How softly blue thy depths appear,
Thy dancing waves, how crystal clear!
How brightly doth the sunlight rest
At last, upon thy quiet breast!
It is because thou liest still—
Submissive to thy Father's will.

So I, at last, give up the strife—
Give up the cherished plans of life;
Yield every hope, each wild desire,
And quench ambition's burning fire.
When lo! my chains no longer gall,
My toils no longer fruitless fall;
And, in the place of storms, is given
The everlasting calms of heaven.

—*Newton Bateman.*

In Historic Dalecarlia

Not far from the city of Falun, on a beautiful headland at Lake Runn, is to be found one of the chief attractions for a visit to historic Dalecarlia. It is the old cottage at Ornäs, where, nearly four hundred years ago, Gustavus Vasa was saved, and through him the country, by the heroic act of a noble woman, Barbro Stigsdotter. It was during those unhappy days when the Danish invaders had succeeded, through cunning and deceit, in capturing every stronghold of Sweden, and the tyrannical Christian II ruled the country with unparalleled cruelty. The only man left to whom the stricken land could look for guidance, since ninety of its noblest men had been beheaded at the massacre of Stockholm, was a young noble, Gustavus Ericsson, known afterwards as the King, Gustavus Vasa, the Father of his Country. But, at this time an outlaw, he was hunted like a wild beast, and in the woods of Dalecarlia he concealed himself, like the illustrious Alfred of England. One cold winter's night he came to Ornäs, where, at the home of his old friend, Arendt Persson, he hoped to receive a shelter and refuge. A warm welcome was given him and he was hidden in the upper story of the cottage. Glad of having found a friend to whom he could unfold his plans and look for support in his efforts to save the country, he at once went to sleep. But the price set on his head was too much for his host; another Judas, he went and sold his master for thirty pieces of silver; but when the traitor came back with the pursuers to betray his guest and his country, the cage was empty, the bird had flown, and the world owed another debt of gratitude to noble and heroic womanhood!

Barbro Stigsdotter, the wife of the deceitful Arendt, suspecting her husband's wicked plans, had at once summoned her most faithful servant, Jacob, and as he stood below, with the fastest horse in the stable harnessed to the sleigh, the noble woman, by means of a long towel, lowered Gustavus, the fugitive, to the ground just in time to effect an escape from his pursuers as they entered the room.

The old cottage is preserved in its original form as a precious relic of that troublous period. It is an old-fashioned log house, at least four hundred years old, and contains a large collection of mementoes of Gustavus Vasa and his times. It is interesting to examine the arrows and cross-bows used by the brave Dalecarlians in repulsing the invaders, to try on the heavy iron helmet worn by Gustavus in the war for independence, and to lift the ghastly broadaxe which was used to cut off the heads of the nobles at the blood-bath of Stockholm. But those dismal times of conflict and tyranny are now happily ended, and the sun shines as brightly over Ornäs and its quaint little cottage as ever; while from the upper porch of that time-honored structure Lake Runn, with its green and smiling shores, presents as peaceful and charming a picture as one may ever see.

Hjalmar Sundquist

A Vision of Santa Claus

In a parlor, snug and cosy,
   With its portières and drapery,
   Its mellow, yellow, papery,
     Umbrella shaded light,
Very cheerful, very rosy,
   With a happy smile a-lurking
   Round the lips, and busy working,
     I saw Santa Claus last night.

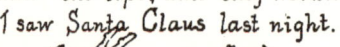

'Twas the saint! A mellow halo
   Just above the head was streaming
   'Twas the saint! 'Twas not dreaming,
     Yet the face was young and fair.
And as low tones from the cello
   Thrill us like a new evangel,
   So this sweet faced children's angel
     With the silver stranded hair.

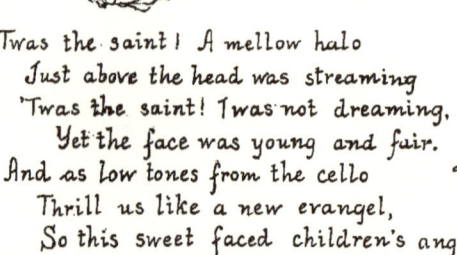

'Twas the saint! The well-known features!
   How the love light streamed in flashes,
   'Neath the silken, sunken, lashes,
     As the busy fingers wrought!
Bead-eyed cotton batting creatures,
   Dainty fairies, starry-wanded,
   Queens and pages, all responded
     To the saints creative thought.

Yes, the children's saint! No other!
Yet should they awake from dreaming
  Of the pale aurora, streaming
    O'er his palace in the North,
They would say to one another,
  "Why, dear me! It's only mother!"
And a little sob would smother,
  As they softly tip-toed forth.

Ah! when some unsealing ointment
  Wakes from every dear illusion,
  And the truth's unasked intrusion
    Shatters every fond ideal,
Like the children's disappointment,
  May ours vanish in the sweeter,
  Higher, holier, completer,
    Nobler glory of the real.

Philip G. & Elizabeth Q. S. Wright.

A Lullaby.

Hush, my little one, hush,
  Whilst the last blush
In the even sky pales in the gloom,
And the last note of the wearied brown thrush
Fills with dream-music the room.

Rest, my little one, rest;
  Whilst in the west
In radiance, the first twilight star
Sheds its pure light o'er the mountain's white crest
Reaching toward splendors afar.

Sleep, my little one, sleep;
  Whilst the winds keep
Watch o'er the blossoms that drowsily fall
Into a sleep that is dreamless and deep,
Waiting the morning's love-call.

Dream, my little one, dream;
  Whilst the first beam
Of the crescent moon falls on the world,
And the star-hosts in the vast heavens gleam,
As night angels' wings are unfurled.

Marie Zetterberg.

THE PLAINT OF THE LEAVES.

One midnight came a mournful wail
   Of voices sobbing low;
I heard the swish of unseen flail
   And then a moan of woe.

But half awake, I thought the sea
   Was breaking on the shore,
Repeating its sad tale to me
   That I'd oft heard before.

Then, peering by the moon's pale light,
   I saw where maples stood,
All shivering in the chilling night
   With never cloak nor hood.

And then I knew the doleful sound
   Was but the plaint of leaves
That lay all stark upon the ground
   Beneath my very eaves.

"O Great Northwind,
"Is't that we've sinned
"We suffer so?
"O, Northwind, O!
"Why is't our lot
"To lie and rot,
"Or on some pyre
"To waste in fire
"That yesterday
"Took those away

"Into the blue
"Whom once we knew?
"O Wind, austere,
"O Wind, we fear
"We've lived in vain,
"We die in pain.
"Is this the end,
"Or shall we spend
"Eternity
"In misery?"

And Northwind said
As o'er his head
He raised his flail
To still their wail:
"I cannot tell
"Or heav'n or hell
"Shall welcome ye;
"By His decree
"I have no rest.
"My constant quest
"Is but to chill
"With death, to kill.
"Yet I'm not sent
"His wrath to vent,
"But restore
"The souls you bore,
"Or saint or knave,
"To Him who gave.
"All scarred and stained
"And there unfeigned
"Each soul shall reach
"His fate to each
"In endless years,
"Of joy or tears."

The Northwind spoke
And then the stroke
Of flail I heard,
But never word
Came from below;
One moan of woe
Escaped to tell
The end; then fell
A cloud's dark pall
Obscuring all.
The Northwind fled
And left his dead
   In peace.

John W. Finley

The Scarf of the Demoiselle

From the French of Jacques Avril.

DURING our last vacation in Normandy, that country where each pebble has its legend and each wood its mystery, we were surprised one day by a storm and took refuge in an old shepherd's cabin, where, picturesquely seated upon his ample cloak, we patiently awaited the end of the shower.

Nothing could be more charming than this unexpected halt in the midst of green meadows with the intoxicating perfume of new-mown hay about us, while the great drops of the heavy summer's rain fell upon the trees with a tinkling sound as of mysterious little bells in the hand of an invisible ringer.

The shower, however, was soon past, and as a magnificent rainbow appeared above the woods across the now clear sky, the old man said, "It is all over, ladies. Do you see the Scarf of the Demoiselle? It is going to be fine now."

"The Scarf of the Demoiselle?" said I, astonished.

"Why yes! the rainbow! We call it the Scarf of the Demoiselle, here." And, without much urging the old shepherd, leaning upon his knotted staff, told us the following touching story:

"One beautiful summer's day, a long, long time ago, people were gleaning in the 'Field of the Demoiselle'; it was a field that belonged in her own right to the daughter of the Castellan, who, since she was very kind, was wont at harvest time to have the sheaves of ripened grain unbound and to allow the poor of the neighboring villages to come and glean. Thus the whole harvest passed into their hands, not a single spike going into the seignorial granaries. She loved to come and visit the gleaners, wearing a simple gown of fine wool and, as her only adornment, a scarf of white silk striped with the seven prismatic colors.

"Now, this day, the oppressive heat presaged a storm, and the young girl was in the field with the gleaners when suddenly great clouds appeared.

"'Hasten my friends,' said she. 'You have only time to reach shelter,' and the gleaners dispersed.

"But behold, yonder, toward the great hedge, appeared a marvelously beautiful young woman, with a veil about her head like the saints in the stained windows of our church. She held by the hand a little child more lovely than the angels, whose fair hair fell rippling over his snow-white robe. The sweet-voiced demoiselle advanced to meet them and, as it was not yet raining, invited them to glean. Both mother and child began to pick up the scattered spikes, laying them in a pile at the end of the field. Meanwhile large drops began to fall, but happily, in a corner near the wood, there was a great spreading oak under which they took refuge; for it was now raining furiously, the thunder rumbled in the distance and lightning flashed across the sky. As the child with his chubby hand raised his mother's veil to shelter his curly head beneath it, the demoiselle took off her scarf and with infinite pains wrapped it about his head and shoulders, placing a kiss upon his brow.

"Then, while the mother smiled sweetly, birds began to sing, and mysterious voices, so tender and pure that human ear had never heard anything like them, filled the air with an invisible and harmonious chorus. At the same time the rain ceased, the clouds disappeared and the demoiselle suddenly noticed that her companions were no longer at her side.

"She seemed to hear the passing of wings, and at the very spot where they had appeared, she saw the child and his mother gently rising upon fleecy clouds, surrounded by angels with azure wings and rosy-pinioned cherubim, all singing a glad hosanna as they mounted into the blue sky.

"Near the horizon they stopped, and as the demoiselle, who had recognized the Virgin and Child Jesus, knelt upon the damp grain in mute adoration, the angels chanted in loud, clear tones, 'Blessed be, Blessed be the good Demoiselle, so kind to the unfortunate! Blessed be the Field of Charity!' The Virgin extended her hands in a gesture of benediction; the Child took from his fair head the scarf and gave its ends to two cherubim who flew out of sight bearing it in opposite directions. It grew in the infinite expanse of the heavens until it formed an immense and marvelous triumphal arch, beneath which, to the sound of celestial music soft and sweet as the sighing of the wind through the woods, passed the Virgin and her Son, followed by the choir of angels and cherubim.

"Then all disappeared.

"But when the young girl arose, in place of a few scattered heads she saw a new harvest standing upright, as abundant as it was miraculous, and the little pile left by the divine gleaners had become a large and lofty stack. The wondrous scarf still shone resplendent in the sky.

"Since that time, after storms, wherever there are kind and generous souls God allows the Scarf of the Demoiselle to appear before the astonished eyes of men, in memory of the good chatelaine."

"But," said I, as the old shepherd finished his tale, "the rainbow is older than that; it dates from the deluge."

"Oh yes," replied the old man, shaking his hoary head, "yes, for learned men who read the Bible, and for the inhabitants of the land where Noah's ark stopped; but we of the West think this story more beautiful; we believe it firmly; and all our old people will tell you that the rainbow is simply the Scarf of the Demoiselle, placed in the sky by the infant Jesus, and held there by two angels of the good God." MARY C. HURD.

On the floor, along the hall,

Rudely traced upon the wall,

There are proofs in every kind —Eugene Field.

Of the havoc they have wrought, March 15, 1892.

And upon my heart you'd find

Just such trademarks, if you sought.

Oh how glad I am 'tis so,

Pittypat and Tippytoe!

"All day long they come and go,"

Pittypat and Tippytoe

and
So wrote one not long ago,

And my little ones at play,
Live this over day by day.
Little Daisy, dimpled, fat,
Claims the name of "Pillypat;"
While gentle Paul, soft and low,
Calls himself my "Tippytoe."

II

"All day long they come and go,
Pittypat and Tippytoe."
Could the tender poet know
All my wee ones' busy day?
Did he see my babes at play?
Did he hear their frequent call
For lost bat or truant ball?
How knew he the weal or woe
Of "Pittypat and Tippytoe"?

"All day long they come and go."

III

"All day long they come and go,—
Pittypat and Tippytoe."
Ever patt'ring to and fro,
Full of mischief as the elves;
None more blithesome than themselves.
Full of frolic, riot, rout,
Ever leaving trace about
Of their presence as they go,—
"Pittypat and Tippytoe."

Footprints up and down the hall,

Playthings scattered on the floor,

Fingermarks along the wall,

Tell-tale streaks upon the door—

IV

"All day long they come and go,—
Pittypat and Tippytoe,"
Back and forward, to and fro.
And they wander in their play,
"Over the Hills and Far Away,"
Staying 'neath "The Sugar Plum Tree,"
Where "Dinkey-Bird" and "Fiddle-Dee-Dee"
Sing "So, So, Rock-a-By So,"
To Pittypat and Tippytoe."

V

"All day long they come and go,
Pittypat and Tippytoe,"
Glad with love and life's warm glow.
Dancing thro' "Good-Children Street"
With light hearts, and happy feet;
Thro' the sunshine, into shade
By the "Fimfalula" made,
Where they "Swing High and Swing Low,"
Pittypat and Tippytoe."

Swing high and swing low
While the breezes they blow;
It's off for a sailor thy father would go.

VI

"All day long they
come and go,—
Pittypat and
Tippytoe,"
Till night hides the
sunset glow.
Then they take the
"Shut-Eye Train,"
Begging for a sweet
refrain
From the songs they love
the best.
And I lull them
to their rest,
Till the "Rock-a-By
Lady slow
Steals "Pittypat
and
Tippytoe."

"The Rock-a-By Lady from Hush-a-By street,
With poppies that hang from her head to her feet;
Then shut your two eyes that are weary, my sweet."

VII.

"All day long they come and go,—
Pittypat and Tippytoe,"
With their hearts now full of woe
For their poet friend at rest,

Sleeping in "God's Acre" blest.
And they beg me bring the chime
Of this feeble little rhyme,
For the one beloved so
By "Pittypat and Tippytoe."

— * Clara * Gordon * Coulson. * —

The Brownies on our Street.

The Brownies have been in Galesburg. Late in October, when the yellow and golden-brown leaves were falling thick and fast from the maples, they came one night to North Academy Street. The beautiful leaves lay in great heaps along the gutters on each side of the way. This meant fun for the Brownies, for they struck their flints and made the sparks fly until the leaves caught fire and the flames went racing up the road.

The people who live along that street saw a weird and pretty picture if they took the trouble to look from their windows that night. The little Brownies laughed and chattered and danced about the bright flames. They flourished their rakes and swung their brooms.

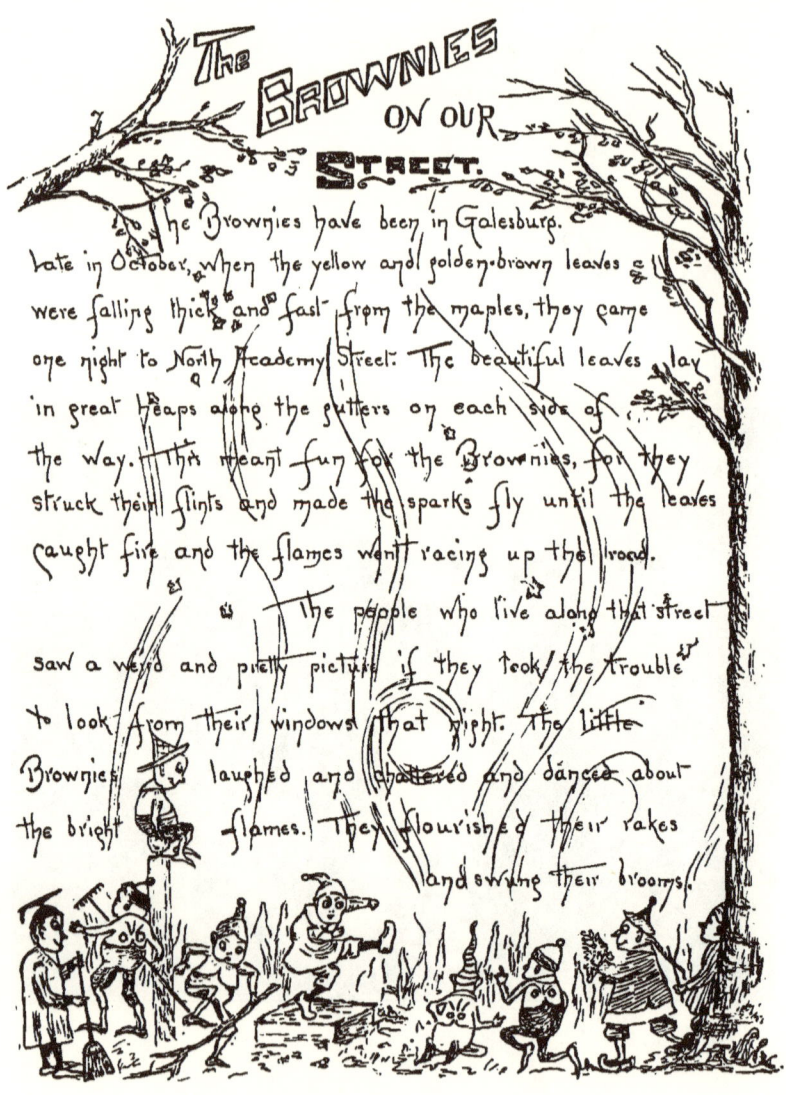

They beat the fire with sticks to keep it from killing the grass. They mounted the hitching posts and danced upon the horse blocks. The glowing flames lighted up the leaves that were still on the trees till they shone like great golden domes.

When the people who had sat about their lamps with drawn shades looked out of their windows the next morning they saw only a long trail of ashes where the deep drifts of leaves had lain the night before. Then they knew that the Brownies had once more begun their fall housecleaning and that it would soon be THANKSGIVING.

NOTE—The Student Brownie is a Galesburg habitant.

Little Things.
Little drops of water,
Little grains of sand,
Make the mighty ocean
And the pleasant land.

So the little moments
Humble tho' they be,
Make the mighty ages
Of Eternity!

So our little errors
Lead the soul away
From the path of virtue,
Far in sin to stray.

The first verse was written the evening previous, in "A Letter to Sabbath School Children."

Little deeds of kindness,
Little words of love,
Help to make earth happy,
Like the Heaven above.
1845.   Julia A. Fletcher.

Tremont Temple,
Boston, Mass.
An exercise at teacher's
morning class in
Pitman's Phonography.

Julia A. Fletcher Carney.
1889

Lincoln at Gettysburg.

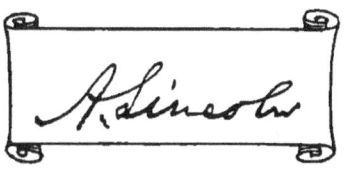

On a bright November afternoon, when the autumn leaves were tinged with a thousand hues of beauty, upon an eminence in the midst of a great plain bounded by lofty mountains, I saw a vast concourse of men and women. I saw among them illustrious warriors, gifted poets, and profound statesmen. I saw ambassadors of mighty empires, governors of great commonwealths, ministers of cabinets, men of high position and power. I saw above their heads, upon every hand, a starry banner, drooping under the weight of sombre drapery. I saw men and women standing among new made graves, overwhelmed with grief which they vainly endeavored to conceal. I knew that I was in the midst of a people bowing under great affliction, of a land stricken with sorrow. I knew that the tide of destruction and death had not ceased to ebb and flow, but that at that moment the fate of my country was trembling in the balance,—her only hope in the fortitude and valor of her sons who were baring their breasts to storms of shot and shell only a few miles away.

I saw standing in the midst of that mighty assembly a man of majestic but benignant mien, of worn and haggard features, but whose eyes beamed with purity, with patriotism, and with hope. Every eye was directed towards him;

and as men looked into his calm, sad, earnest face, they recognized the great President, the foremost man of the world, not only in position and power but in all the noblest attributes of humanity. When he essayed to speak, such solemn silence reigned as when, within consecrated walls, men come into the presence of Deity. Each sentence, slowly and earnestly pronounced, sank into every patriotic heart, gave a strange lustre to every face, and nerved every arm. In those utterances, the abstract, the condensation, the summing up of American patriotism, were contained the hopes, the aspirations, the stern resolves, the consecration, the dedication upon the altar of humanity, of a great people.

From the time of that solemn dedication the final triumph of the loyal hosts was assured. As the Christian day by day repeats the solemn words of prayer given him by his Savior, so the American Patriot will continue to repeat those inspired sentiments. While the Republic lives he will continue to repeat them, and while, realizing all their solemn significance, he continues to repeat them, *the Republic will live.* CLARK E. CARR.

AN EVERGREEN

ACT I.

A boy and girl standing in the door of a tiny chalet at Grindelwald.

Girl. Ach Hans! Do you see the small tree? Mutter, Mutter, come here! There's a new baby tree in the snow.

Mother. [*From within*] Play by yourselves, Kinder. I'm hard pressed by the work.

Boy. A tree's not so much to see. The valley's full of them.

Girl. [*Stooping over a young evergreen near by, and whispering to it*] I've seen you, little tree, and I know you must be awfully cold. My toes are always cold all winter, but it is most time for the sun to shine 'round this corner and then you'll feel so beautiful. [*She runs into the house and returns with two pieces of bark. Puts the bark up about the tree*] This will keep off the wind, and I'll pile the snow all around your roots. You can be my tree now and I'll take care of you.

ACT II.

The Tree. Ach! the sun's rays have kissed me. The Mädchen is so good to send the sun this way. My roots have not pressed forward far, for the ground is very cold and hard. Ach! I'm shivering so. That wind which comes to chill me must be straight from the glacier behind the Kinder's chalet. My Mädchen was very kind to tell me that it was spring-time now, but the spring winds are sehr kalt. Ach! 'tis the Mädchen's voice!

Girl comes out of the chalet, knitting a small blue sock and singing slowly:

    I'm coming to you, O tree! O tree!
        Yo—del—yo—del,
    I'm coming to you, O tree!
        Yo—del—yo—del.

Himmel! the poor tree! The harsh wind has torn the bark away, and your poor branches are twisting all about, and there's a pile of snow on you, too. [*Brushes snow off and re-arranges the shelter. Sits down beside the tree; her knitting drops in her lap and she puts her arms about the tree*] Ach! my little tree, I'm sore distressed. The Mutter beat me this day. Yes, 'twas schiver. She took the Alpenstock from the chest where it rests and she struck me the full force of the Stock three times. I can't show you how it was; 'twould hurt you so. Ach! 'twould hurt you so, mein Baum. You see, Hans and I were up to see if the glacier was melting, for the Vater said last night that the water would be coming down in torrents from the mountains. But torrents there were not—just a wee bit of a stream that you could hardly spy. Hans pushed me once and the crevasse nigh swallowed me up. Hans told the Mutter and then she stocked me, because I'm the first-born and ought to know better. I'm so glad that you're the weest tree in the valley, or the other trees might stock you. [*Buries her head in the branches.*

Mother. [*Calling from the door*] Gretchen! Gretchen! There's the wood to fetch.

Girl. [*Jumping up*] Ach, so. I must go to her.

ACT III.

SCENE I.

THREE MONTHS LATER.

The Tree. The summer is my love and the sweet sun claims her, too. Ach! but I care not; I share the warmth of each. Warm! everything is warm in summer. I shake my green branches and the warm air floats all about me. Even the sound of the rushing glacier-stream is warmed before it reaches my ears. Himmlische warmth! Even when I look at the snow afar off on the mountain tops, I realize the more how warm I am. I am so happy, so snug and warm.

SCENE II.

Boy and girl picking berries in the valley. Sudden sound like thunder in the mountains as an avalanche comes tearing down.

 Boy. [*Stopping work and looking 'round*] There's a smacking somewhere; isn't that a jolly rumble?
 Girl. [*Picking berries*] Hans! Hans! Perhaps it killed somebody.
 Hans. Killed the Kuh.
 Girl. My basket's full. [*Takes both baskets*] Let's come and sit under my Baum, and eat the berries. [*Starting to run*] First there, gets the biggest basket.
 They run up the valley and see all the pastures on one side of the chalet covered with snow; the chalet itself is half buried in a mass of snow and ice.
 Girl. [*Dropping baskets*] The Mutter! Ach, Hans! the Mutter!
 Boy rushes wildly toward back of house, which is barricaded by snow. With a terrified scream, he turns suddenly and sees his mother, who is searching for her children and calling loudly.
 Boy. Ach, Mutter! We're here!

Mother. Und die Schwester?

They look and see the sister riveted to the spot where she stood, the berries all spilled about her.

Mother. Gretchen! Gretchen! come here.

Girl. [*Bursting into tears and throwing herself on the ground*] Mein Baum! Ach! Mutter! My Liebchen is dead!

Boy. It's fitter if you didn't cry for your tree when the Mutter and I are alive.

Girl. Ach! The cruel Summer!

HELENA CRUMETT-LEE.

THE PASSING OF CADMVS

There's a new-made shrine deserted;
    There's a tripod overturned;
There's an oracle perverted,
    And its patron saint is spurned.

From the ecumenic roster
    They've erased the best of all;
And the rampant, piebald poster—
    They have turned it to the wall.

In that vacant bookshop corner
    Cadmi erstwhile joyed to meet;
Now the sacrilegious scorner
    Occupies the window seat.

Once to wear the Cadmean habit
    Was our unrestricted wish,
When the Welsh was on the rabbit
    And the chafe was on the dish.

From our strength there came forth sweetness;
    From the eater came forth meat;
Now the club has lost completeness;
    If we meet we simply eat.

So proud Cadmus deemed us vandals;
   Girded up his traveling gown;
Shook our dust from off his sandals;
   Shook his head, and "shook" the town.

Still the Hawthorne brews Young Hyson;
   Still Mosaic "moseys" on;
And the old world's broad horizon
   Still sticks out with their renown.

Still Euterpean doth glad us;
   Still Fortnightly doth confer;
But the Club of good Saint Cadmus
   Is among the things that were.
EARNEST ELMO CALKINS.

THE FIR TREE

From the German of Friedrich Adolf Geissler.

N THAT holy night when the Saviour was born in Bethlehem, and the heavenly hosts carried the glad news to the shepherds, God sent one of His heralds to the German land to carry the great tidings to the world that was wrapped in winter.

The snow hung heavily upon the branches of the trees. It was bitter cold, and the trees all slept. But the angel awakened

them with the message that Christ, The Holy One, was born.

"I know him not," said the powerful oak; "it was only yesterday morning that Wotan's priest, standing under my branches, offered a steed to the Father of the gods. The warm blood was spattered upon my trunk; and see,—there hangs the head of the sacrifice. From out the roaring of my leaves Wotan speaks to the races of men; who is greater than he?"

"I know him not," said the linden; "I am rooted deep in German ground; I look afar over German lands; what care I for him who is born in a foreign land?"

"Wonderful tidings you bring," said the aspen mockingly; "you tell us in this cold winter night of a new eternal life? I stretch my bare branches out into the air; and then I am to believe your words? Let this God whom you announce clothe me with foliage, and let the fir tree here bear sweet fruit; then will I believe what you tell us."

The angel turned to the fir tree. But she was silent; for she was filled with awe, and reverently bowed her slender form before the messenger of God. And the angel breathed upon her; and behold,—the heavy snow melted from her branches; and the little fir tree was adorned with sweet fruits.

The naked boughs of the aspen were covered with foliage; but the young leaves trembled and quivered before the great wonder that had come to pass.

And the angel said, "Thy leaves shall always tremble, to remind thee of thy mockery. But thou, dear believing fir, shalt be a happy tree. As often as the holy night descends upon the earth shall thy branches bear fruits and sweet things, so that everyone who rejoices in thee shall be reminded of the wonderful mystery of Christmas night.

And such a tree the Christ Child makes ready for you on Christmas eve. Steal quietly into the room some time when the candles are burnt out and sit alone under its branches and it will tell you its own story.

ALICE B. CUSHING.

The Meteor

From the realms of starry light
  Out of darkness into night.
Like a Lucifer thou'rt cast
  Out of present into past.

  What message, stranger, from above,
    Bring'st thou from the God of Love,
  Who the universe creates
    Who existence dominates?

Wer't thou traitor to his trust,
  Thus to be from heaven thrust,
Or wer't thou from Elysium hurled
To founder, be of some new world?

  Has thy mission been fulfilled,
    That thy fevered life is stilled,
    Or in creations plan divine,
      Is some usefulness yet thine?

Solved not is thy gleaming being,
  None knows where thou'rt flashing, fleeing,
Trackless are the paths thou'st trod,
  Rests thy mystery with God.   Frankie Hinckley Sisson

A REVERIE BY THE HEATHER

A bit of Heather from Bonnie Scotland

Ay, ay, what dreams hae I had a' thae years! Dreams o' the land—if not my ain—still, land o' my fathers. But what a hazy mirage is my rosiest dream compared wi' what mi' ain een look on the day!

Resting on this heathery knowe,—ahint me, the rashy howe, the whinstane hedge, the specks o' green, the near and distant fields o' bonnie, purple heather. Afore me, the tiny, thorn-bounded fields o' yellowing corn, the deep, green grass, where erstwhile bloomed the "wee, modest, crimson-tipped flow'r;" yon thicket o' bracken, yon rustling wood, yon glen wha's stony braes gie unco scant fare to the hazel and the rowan tree, yon burn wha's peat-stained waters rush noisily past the wee thack biggin and bid me say with its peasant poet:

> "Whyles ower a linn the burnie plays,
>   As thro' the glen it wimples;
> Whyles roun' a rocky scaur it strays,
>   Whyles in a weil it dimples."

Nearby, a whinny knowe wi' its ruined keep, its crumbling wa's wi' ivy clad. And at its foot the sleepy clachen, quaint and hoary; the auld, auld Kirk, wha's meenister ever renews its "Auld, Auld Story;" and the moss-grown slabs whaur "the rude forefathers of the clachen sleep." One modest shaft sentineled by a haw tree tells that here fell and rests ane o' thae saints frae wha's simple life and martyr's death "Auld Scotland's grandeur springs."

But I maun gang. The sun lang syne's gane doon ahint Knockdohan's sombre dome, the mavis chants his evening song, 'tis noo "atween the gloamin' and the mirk," and, tho' enchanted by nature's simple, rural beauty, yet my heart aye fondly turns tae a spot—if indeed no fairer, yet dearer—a prairie hame over the sea.

JANET GREIG.

To the Daisy

Fresh and green was the meadow and
 bathed in the dew
  of the morning,
Covered with wild field
 daisies, white as the
  snow, that in winter
Clothes the earth in a shroud of white, of fair
  and ethereal beauty.
Oh! sweet and magical daisy, what secrets
  are hidden within you!
Oft have your snow-white petals been plucked
  by the hands of the children,—
Plucked from their golden crown, to tell the
  fortunes of children;
Strewn in the grassy pathway, trampled and
  crushed by the children.

— Marie Zetterberg.

An Immortelle.

A fresh pink bud,
All rosy like the morn,
Grew on my sill
The day our babe was born.
At first, all close
The petals round did press
Its fragrant heart,
And we could only guess
Of what was hid
Within each veined cell
Of rose and white.
Still did the sweet bud swell.
The glowing sun
Each day tried all his power
To open it,
To make the bud a flower.
My wonder grew;
I watched it hour by hour.
I did not know
The name of my sweet flower.
One of God's winds
Had dropped the little seed
Into the earth
All fitted for its need.
At last the bud
Burst in a sheaf
Of crimson bloom.
Each ruddy, fragrant leaf,
Instinct with life,
Answered my question well.
I knew my flower—
It was an Immortelle.

Close in my arms
My little baby lies.
I can but guess
What lies behind those eyes
So deep and blue.
All trustful is the gaze
Which meets my own.
I watched for many days
My bud unfold
Its petals to the sun
Of loving smiles.
Full swift the days move on —
The great eyes look
Some faint, far sound   With recognition sweet
To tell my mother-love   Into my own.
What flower will come   A dimpled smile will greet
From baby-bud. Above   And answer mine.
The clouds, a Voice   My eager eyes would peer
Of Christly tenderness —   Beyond the now —
"The little ones   Wistful I bend to hear
Suffer to come to Me,
It is of such
My kingdom great shall be."
I bow my head —
Christ's self hath
answered well
My questionings —
I have an
Immortelle!

Annie
Bateman
Ewart.

57

"To struggle, to seek, to find,
and never to fail."
—*Nansen.*

The Home-Coming Of ❧ ❧ ❧ Thorstein Ericsson

The Norsemen were nearing home. For many a day had the rowers toiled hardily at the oars of ash. Day in, day out, as they stood their shifts at the sweeps, had they listened to the wash of the waves against the black sides of the staunch Sea-Otter, had watched the brine-drops glistening in the sun-light with the dripping of the oars. But now were the sweeps hauled in-boards; and the sea-farers lolled idly on the rowing-benches, while the great sail tugged at the sheets, filling and bellying as it caught the wind,—the wind that was driving the sea-rover on a fair course; now the carved otter's head at the prow climbed the slope of a rising wave, now it plunged with a silvery dash of spray adown the slant of sunlit sea. With Leif, son of Eric, and his thirty-five sea-fellows had all happed luckily. In the hold a rare lading of timber; on deck, tongues atremble with tales of marvel, of searching and finding, of striving and mastery,—thus were the vikings homeward-bound, and in every man was the heart light. Along the sea-line, across the blue plain of swelling tide, foam-flecked, lay a haze that was neither cloud-land nor fog-bank nor rising mist; for here and there brightly gleamed, as with the whiteness of flame, some peak where the ice-cap caught the sun. This was Greenland, and one day's faring more must bring the Otter safe into Ericsfirth where lay the homestead of their kin. Therefore were the Norsemen blithe.

"Ho, Thorstein, son of Eric," cried one of a group of shipmen sky-larking in the waist. "Cease thy moody dreamings and sing us some brave strain of the home-land. Since dawn hast thou been as glum as a drabbled crow in a rain-storm; tune up, friend mine, and let not the wind now do all the piping."

"Dost need to be sung at, Tyrker?" lazily answered a handsome, dark-haired youth, by half-a-head the tallest of the men on ship-board; leaning against the mast, with arms carelessly folded over his broad chest, he had indeed been staring unwittingly toward the shore, while the sharp prow rose and sank with the easy swell. "Yes, Thorstein; a song, a song!" came the clamor of the group; for Thorstein, Leif's Brother, was a scald of some fame, and had the favor of men second only to Leif himself.

"Why, thou freckle-faced pigmy," laughed Thorstein, making as if to hurl a thwart-iron at Tyrker, who was short of body and somewhat misshapen and ugly, albeit stout of limb and fond of sport. "Thou dwarf-child; didst sing a song of thine own once on a time. I heard thee chattering and chanting, thy tongue thick with the juice of the wine-berries thou hadst stored. Hast forgotten, O Tyrker?—thy ship-fellows have not;"—and truly a great laughter did straightway arise from the crowd; and sounded loudest of all the hoarse voice of Tyrker, for he was a good-natured carl and even when drunk was more like to sing than to fight, which tickled the Northmen for it worked otherwise with them; but Tyrker was from the South.

" 'Tis a true word, brother mine," spoke now Leif, the Earl, who had come forward from the after-deck where the steersman stood, and where Leif Ericsson the most-while staid. " 'Tis a true word; and well I mind me of the song friend Tyrker sang the day we first met the Skralings. Dost remember, Tyrker, the speed of thy footings over the sand-dunes? 'Twas a merry tune thou gavest us betwixt thy breathings and thy heavings. By my shield, Tyrker, I bethought me of my old hound, Wolf; thy pantings and thy howlings were the very same, only I think thy little-legged body rolled over the ground more fleetly than ever Wolf had made it."

Another burst of laughter, and when it was past, Tyrker, with his face a little awry, took up the word for himself.

"True, foster-son, mine," said he. "I did let the Skralings see my heel-play on the sand-hills, and mayhap 'twas no love-song thou heardest old Tyrker yelp when he was near enough to reach thine ear. And I bethink me that had there been no dog, Tyrker, to bark at thee that day, thou and thy northern men might now be asleep in Wineland yonder, stead of home-sailing in Sea-Otter, and gibing thy foster-father for that he is short and ugly whilst thou and thy scape-grace kinsman there be tall and lithe. Nay—I be not angry, Leif," he cried, seeing a look in the Earl's face, "never angry with thee or Thorstein, Leif Ericsson; too much I love thee both ever to feel hard toward either of thee."

"And if there were wine-juice left in the ship, old Tyrker, thou shouldst have thy fill," cried Leif. "In very sooth, there is no man here more faithful, foster-father, than thou, and thou must take in good part what thy comrades put on thee; 'tis a sign of their love for thee, and thou knowest right well what my brother Thorstein and I think."

"Make not a quarrel over my folly, good Tyrker," said Thorstein, pushing his way to the old man on whose freckled face once more danced the laugh-light, "and to repay the gibe, shalt have the song thou askedst for; it shall tell the tale of the Norsemen's faring; and I call it the 'Song of Leif, the Happy.'" "But not now, brother," said Leif, "for here is work to do." And it was so that ere this the Earl, who was in all things best, in eye-sight and in head-work first of all, had seen from the steerage a strange hap. "I think," said Leif, "that yonder is either a ship, or a skerry; and there be men thereon."

And so it proved; for Leif Ericsson was in all ways truly safe leader, and in this sea-faring there came to him much wealth and great fame. Now when the ship neared the skerry, behold fifteen folk stood upon the cliff and they seemed to be in need of help. Called Leif to Tyrker: "O Tyrker, take two men with thee in the skiff and go, ask how this folk fare and what they will."

And when the Otter had come so near as was safe to the skerry, then put forth Tyrker in the small boat; and the land-folk came swiftly down a foot-way that led to sea-shore and stood there with their belongings. Now it was a waste land and barren of trees and rocky between the sea and the hill-country, so that the Northmen marvelled that men should be there, and this the more when they saw that in the crowd were two women. By this the small boat was come within hail, and Tyrker called to the leader of the group, "Friend, who art thou—and hast thou need?" "I am called Thorer," said the man on shore, "and I am of northern kin; in sooth we have need and I pray you to take us hence, for there hath been ship-wreck; we be houseless and foodless, and shall starve, happen we get not help from you. But who be thy ship-fellows?"

"We be Leif Ericsson's men and the Earl bids you and your folk to come aboard ship if ye have need," said Tyrker. Then came the guests aboard the Otter. Now there were with Thorer, who was also Earl, Gudrid his wife and their daughter, Freydis; and twelve men beside who were serving-men and fighters; and had been storm-driven on that beach and had suffered some days. So, right glad were they of Leif's offer.

But the women were aweary and some-deal faint; thus it happed that Tyrker, who was an awkward man at handling women and ever uncouth, let slip the maid so that she nigh fell betwixt the skiff and the ship's side; yet haply stood Thorstein by the gunwale, who quickly reached forth with his hands and caught Freydis, and she lay fainting in Thorstein's arms.

Now Freydis was the fairest maid that ever had Thorstein seen. White like cream was her skin, and her hair that hung low down was like burnished copper when the sun shineth on it. Moreover she was shy before the menfolk and spake with her mother only, and this seemed grievous to Thorstein. But once he would go to Leif who stood with the steersman on the after-deck, where also sat the women and Thorer; and when the youth about-faced on his stride, lo, the eyes of the maiden were turned toward his place; bethought Thorstein never had he seen a look so sweet in maiden's eye before. Yet it seemed that Freydis saw not Thorstein, only the sea and the land beyond; wherefore he heard her say plainly: "There, O mother mine,—*there* is home; happy is Freydis thy daughter, happy, happy!" and Gudrid kissed the maid. Belike they saw not the fading of the brightness from his face.

That night because the wind held fair and there was no need to row, Thorer's troop were joined with Leif's men in a merry-making near the fore-castle, while Thorer talked with Leif at the stern and the two women sat leaning on the thwarts and listened, resting. Then spoke Tyrker among the shipmen: "Now, Thorstein, foster-son, let us hear that song thou wottest of; that 'Song of Leif the Happy,' I think thou calledst it." "The song, the song!" cried all. "Nay, I cannot sing," said Thorstein, moodily. "*Brrr!*" grunted Tyrker; "be not so surly. Hast a good voice and a fine wit; never knew I thee to be thus unmannerly nor whimsical before. I pray thee let us hear thee sing."

"And if I sing, it will not please thee, Tyrker", said Thorstein more gently. "For the song thou wouldst hear, that I cannot sing: and what I will to sing, that is of a sort that toucheth not thy liking; nevertheless, and as thou wilt." Then Thorstein sang:

"The white-winged sea-gull seeks the shore;
  There are storms out on the deep.
I hear the hoarse-toned rollers roar,—
  Fear not, fair lady, sleep;
    Fear not, but sleep!

"The raven swart now seeks the nest;
  There's a sobbing in the pines.
My weary soul will know no rest,
  Until its love it finds,--
    Its own love finds!"

Now Thorstein had a strong, sweet voice and it could hardly hap but that they on the after-deck should hear the song. Still Thorer talked with Leif and the maid lay with her head in Gudrid's lap; maybe she was asleep.

When Thorstein had thus far sung the lay, broke Tyrker rudely in; "Now saidst thou more truly than I deemed, ship-fellow, when thou didst give warning that thy song should not please. Such Frankish love-lays like me not. Better love I such brave chantings as the wandering Saxon brought to Brattalid; fine tales he sang of Hrothgar's Hall, and the stout sword-play of Hygelac's thane. But what aileth thee, friend Thorstein? the whole day's while hast thou been mooning and glooming with thyself. May thy name-god strike me stark with his hammer but since thou fondled yonder maid ——"

What Tyrker had yet on his tongue to say he finished not yet, and in good sooth it is a marvel he said ever aught beside; whereas in that moment Thorstein's short-sword flashed in the blue moon-light, and the haft struck Tyrker's skull that the old man shut his little eyes, and his white teeth cracked and crunched. "My name-god gives thee greeting, Tyrker," said Leif's brother; "and his hammer he still keeps for a while."

Thorstein strode aft to where his brother talked with Thorer. Loud rang the laughter of the carls as Tyrker limped surlily toward the forecastle, muttering and shaking, whiles he rubbed his broken poll; yet what was in his mind he spake not aloud.

"Well, good Thorstein," said Earl Thorer, "wilt thou, too, go a-faring like thy brother when the summer be come again?" "Nay," said the youth, "that cannot I now tell; first is for me a quest near-by home; fail I in that quest, it may well be that I fare sea-ward before the summer."

Now Thorer looked askance, but Leif, who was ever sharp-sighted, deemed Thorstein's riddle to be no riddle to him; thus he smiled, but spake naught.

That night was the moon large and shining like a piece of new silver freshly rubbed, and for a while were they all quiet. But when the women went to their resting-place below deck, went down first Leif, to show the way, and after him followed Thorer and next Gudrid came; so it happed that the younger woman lingered for a while, looking on the sea. Then said Thorstein: "Maid, wilt help me in my quest?" Yet was Freydis silent; only whiles she stood before the youth, she raised her eyes, slow and shy, to Thorstein's eyes, that he looked straight into them; and the moon-light shone upon the maid's face that him-seemed to know of nothing half so fair on earth. "And if I do not know what the quest may be—my lord?" said Freydis.

With the dawn was great gladness on the Otter, whereas they were now near-by home. Then sailed the Northmen gaily with singing of sea-songs and with shouting and smiting of blade and brand, into that bay that is called Ericsfirth; and behold, Eric the Red and all the kin-folk were upon the beach, and there they brought the Viking-ship to haven, and there was feasting and great mirth; but among the kindred was no man blither, says the tale, than Thorstein Ericsson. W. E. SIMONDS.

LITTLE FOOTSTEPS

In the snow around my door
Many footprints may be seen:
Of the larger, many score,
But sweet tiny ones between.
O, but I do love them so,—
Little footsteps in the snow.

Morning footsteps point away,
And the snow is lightly pressed:
Heavily, at close of day,
Trudge the little feet to rest;
Stress their dragging outlines show,
Little footsteps in the snow.

Once again they'll leave my side,
Soon those feet will eager roam.
Father, grant, at eventide
Weary, they may turn toward home,
As homeward turned, so long ago,
Those little footsteps in the snow.

Lee S. Pratt.

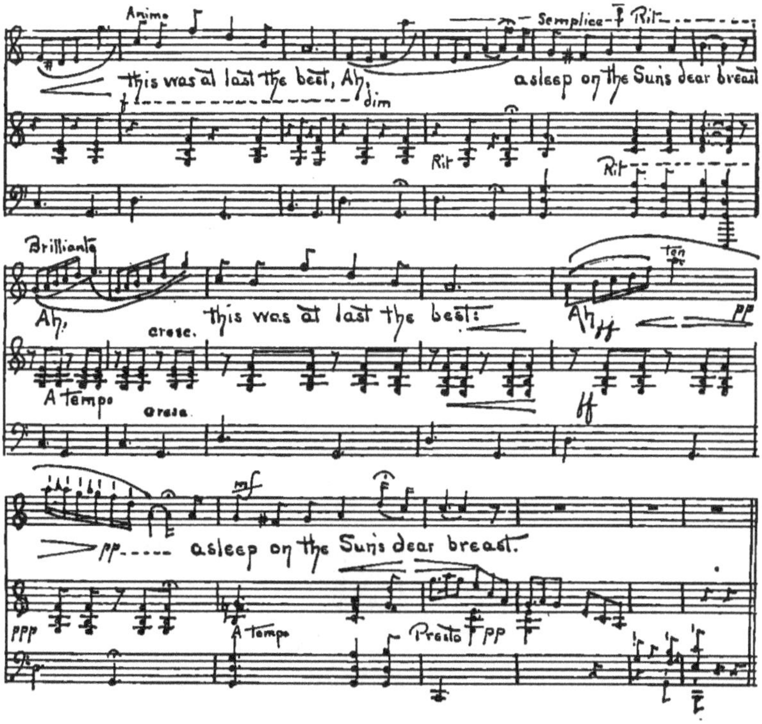
Animo
Semplice
Rit
this was at last the best, Ah,
dim
asleep on the Suns dear breast
Rit
Rit
Brilliante
Ah,
cresc.
this was at last the best:
ten
Ah,
ff
pp
A tempo
Cresc.
ff
pp
asleep on the Suns dear breast.
mf
ppp
A tempo
Presto
pp

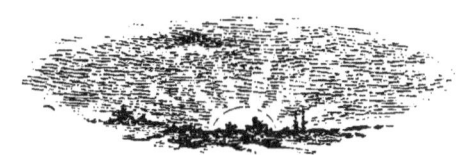

"There are as many fine fish in the ocean as ever before were caught."

This page stands in honor of those numerous authors of unquestioned talent, Galesburg's Miltons, mute (as far as these pages are concerned) but not inglorious, who in some brighter day and a future edition — shall yet give forth their writings — to the world.

"All things come to him who Waits."

Notes:

The "Tribute to the Flag," is a reproduction of the first three pages of a lecture on our "Duty to the Government," delivered in Knox Chapel, May 20, 1886. It was written in ink, whereas most of the Doctor's manuscripts are in pencil.

When the editor began to collect material for the "Sketches," Dr. Bateman was waylaid one morning as "Old Ned" was slowly propelling him along Losey Street. After various pleasantries had passed, the plan of the book was broached, in which the Doctor was greatly interested; but when a proposition was made for the "Outside Seat" incident, he laughed heartily, tho' would only say, "We'll see." The next time the matter was urged, he asked quizzically, "Do you really want to have that old thing, Professor?" The aid of his niece was then invoked, and she was allowed several days in which to secure the coveted privilege; and, even then, when the editor called at "The Farm" for the final decision, Miss Lee followed Dr. Bateman into seclusion whence he had retreated, but soon returned with the triumphant reply that 'the little uncle' would grant the request." Soon the "little uncle" himself appeared, in his happiest mood, and with many a gay repartee received the thanks that greeted the announcement. Alas, that this should be the final interview! On the afternoon and evening before Dr. Bateman's death, he spent several hours searching for the desired lecture, as his niece afterwards said, stopping only with the dusk. A pile of manuscripts of California lectures found on his desk testified to the thoroughness of the quest. The episode of the race, as he relates it, displays a side of the good Doctor's character that we all knew and loved.

The poem of Dr. Bateman's quoted here is the conclusion of the lecture in which the race for the outside seat is so charmingly told. The day after that incident he went with a party of friends to "Pebble Beach," at Pescadero; and during the afternoon he made his way, alone, to a cleft in the rocks of a promontory projecting far out into the sea. "Does not such an afternoon," he exclaims, "give a new meaning to the words, 'Nearer, my God, to Thee?' Should not vanity and littleness and selfishness and meanness and all hatreds and despicableness be drowned to death in such floods? How tempted we are to speak to that mighty personality, so correlate in its passions and its calm to our own! May I confess," he adds, "that I found the temptation irresistible, as I sat alone, in that wonderful presence, on that memorable summer's afternoon."

For the reproductions from Eugene Field given in connection with Mrs. Coulson's poem, a volume of the poet's original manuscripts was kindly loaned by Mrs. Field. The photographs were taken under the editor's personal supervision, the precious book not being allowed out of his sight. In the illustration, "The Sugar-Plum Tree," of the two birds perched upon the limb the one on the left is a redrawing of Mr. Field's idea of "The Dinkey Bird," as sketched by him at the head of the original copy of the poem of that name. The other bird on the limb is supposed to be "Fiddle-Dee-Dee."

"Lincoln at Gettysburg," is taken from the peroration of a Decoration Day address delivered by the Hon. Clark E. Carr at Galesburg, May 30, 1879. Aside from its literary value, it has a distinct historic interest as being the word painting of an eye witness of the immortal scene it portrays. Colonel Carr was a member of the Commission having the Gettysburg ceremonies in charge, and it was at his suggestion that President Lincoln was invited to deliver an address.

The autograph of President Lincoln at the head of this article is a reproduction of a copy generously loaned by his son, the Honorable Robert T. Lincoln, of Chicago. Mr. Lincoln observed that he had but few autographs of his father and that these were all, or nearly all, affixed to bank checks, except the President's signature to his son's commission in the army. The autograph furnished was taken from a bank check made out to an insurance company, and was dated by Abraham Lincoln, "Springfield, Sept. 5, 1860."

The artistic illustrations in Mrs. Cushing's translation are the work of Walter Caspari, a personal friend of hers in Munich. The bit of entree work is by the same talented artist.

To the editor of "The Interior" thanks are due for his courteous permission to use "The Plaint of the Leaves."

The following comment outlines the material upon which is based the Norse Idyl by Professor Simonds: In the royal library at Copenhagen is an ancient manuscript book which contains historic records of the Norsemen until the end of the fourteenth century. That portion of the book which deals with the voyages to America previous to the coming of Columbus, was photographed by royal command and arranged with a translation in a handsome volume for exhibition at the World's Fair of 1893. Only a few copies of this volume exist, and by the kindness of the Hon. Clark E. Carr, to whose interest and effort largely, the very existence of this reproduction is due, one copy found its way to the Knox College Library, where, under the title of "The Flatey Book," it may be seen by all. In the chronicle descriptive of the return voyage from Wineland, occur the following lines:

"Sailed now after that to sea and got fair wind until they saw Greenland and fells under the glaciers; then took a man to speak and quoth to Leif, 'Why steerest thou the ship so much under the wind?' Leif answers, 'I take care of my rudder, but of more than that besides; or what do you see remarkable?' They answered that they saw nothing remarkable. 'I do not know,' said Leif, 'if I see a ship or a skerry [i. e. promontory].' Now they saw it and said it to be a skerry; he saw yet sharper than they, so that he saw men on the skerry. 'Now I will that we beat against the wind,' said Leif, 'so as to get near to them.' * * * Now they sailed to the skerry and let go, cast anchor, and put out another little boat which they had with them. Then Tyrker asked who was the leader of the party. He told himself to be called Thorer and to be of Northern kin; 'but what is thy name?' Leif told it him. 'Art thou son of Eric the Red, of Brattalid,' says he. Leif replied that so he was. 'Now I will,' says Leif, 'bid you all on my ship and those goods that the ship will hold.' They accepted those terms and sailed afterwards to Ericsfirth."

Later it transpires that Thorer's wife, Gudrid, was one of the little company thus rescued by Leif Ericsson; but, strangely enough, the earlier historian makes no mention of Thorer's daughter, Freydis; nor does he deal with numerous other interesting details of the voyage, which, on his part, certainly constitutes a grave neglect of obvious duty. It is therefore to supply some of these deficiencies in the record that this second account of the homecoming of Thorstein Ericsson has been related by Professor Simonds, who declares that there is much more of interest yet to tell, only time and space forbid a longer narrative here.

The heather spray at the head of Miss Greig's "Reverie," is a drawing from a bit of *white* heather received from Scotland within the last few weeks. This kind of heather is very rare and is regarded much as the four-leaved clover is with us, being eagerly sought for as a token of good luck. May it bring an abundant store of that desirable article to every reader of this amiable little book, is the cordial wish of

THE EDITOR.

www.ingramcontent.com/pod-product-compliance
Lightning Source LLC
Chambersburg PA
CBHW020231090426
42735CB00010B/1637